SQUIRE BOONE

Indiana Historical Bureau
From the collection of Frederick P. Griffin

1

Other Books By W. Fred Conway

- **Chemical Fire Engines**
- **Corydon — The Forgotten Battle Of The Civil War**
- **Discovering America's Fire Museums**
- **Firefighting Lore**
- **The Most Incredible Prison Escape Of The Civil War**
- **What The Bible Says About Prehistoric Man**
- **Young Abe Lincoln - His Teenage Years in Indiana**

FBH Publishers
P.O. Box 711, New Albany, IN 47151-0711
Phone 1-800-234-1804

Library of Congress Cataloging in Publication Data
Conway, W. Fred, Sr.

The Incredible Adventures of Daniel Boone's Kid Brother - Squire
Library of Congress Catalog Number: 91-075967
ISBN 0-925165-08-5

FBH Publishers, P.O. Box 711, New Albany, IN 47151-0711
© W. Fred Conway, Sr. 1992 • Second Edition 1994

Typography and Layout: Pam Jones
Maps: Andy Markley
Cover Design: Ron Grunder

The Incredible Adventures of Daniel Boone's Kid Brother —

By W. Fred Conway

Although fame eluded Squire Boone, his daring exploits were no less colorful and dramatic than those of his famous brother.

Of the first eight white men who dared to enter "the dark and bloody ground", as Kentucky was known to the pioneers in the early 1770's, only two returned alive ... brothers Daniel and Squire Boone.

CONTENTS

PREFACE

Squire Boone was a man of many talents. He was a skilled gunsmith, a carpenter, a farmer, a dedicated minister of the Gospel, a builder and operator of gristmills, and a fearless explorer and frontiersman. But, of all his activities, he was best known as an Indian fighter. Early Boone historians referred to Indians as savages, even as bloodthirsty savages. These terms I also have used in recounting Squire's numerous encounters with the red man.

However, I would remind the reader that the Indians were in this land first. They, not the settlers, were the first true owners. We call them American Indians, but they were not Americans until white settlers named their land America. Invaded by men who took over their territory, the Indians used the only methods they knew to try to repel the incursion of the white man - tomahawks, rifles, and treachery. But would white men not have done the same if the circumstances had been reversed?

The author counts among his personal friends a number of native Americans, and nothing in this book is intended to disparage this proud race in any way.

W. Fred Conway

CHAPTER ONE

"ORDAINED BY PROVIDENCE"

The days were growing ever shorter, and the nights ever colder at Daniel and Rebecca Boone's pioneer log cabin in the Yadkin Valley of North Carolina in late November, 1769. However, Daniel wasn't there. He had left on the first day of May on an expedition to try to locate the legendary land known as Kentucky, reputed to be some two hundred miles to the northwest. There, it was said, were deer, buffalo, and beaver without number, with bounteous meadows and cane so thick as to make the land of Kentucky, if it truly existed, a veritable paradise.

Seven long months had now passed since Daniel Boone had set out on his quest to find the fabled land of plenty; and in all that time no word had come from him. Daniel was thirty-five years old when he left behind his wife Rebecca and their seven children and began his exploration into the unsettled lands toward the northwest. Various others from the valley had left with him, including his brother-in-law, John Stewart, who was married to his sister Hannah. Rebecca and Hannah were sick with worry over their husbands. Someone would have to leave in search of them before winter closed its snowy and icy grip on the area known not only as Kentucky, but as the "Dark and Bloody Ground."

"I'll go," spoke up a young man, whose fondness and admiration for his older brother was well known among the pioneers of North Carolina's Yadkin Valley. The volunteer was Squire Boone, who at age twenty-five was Daniel's youngest brother. Squire looked fondly at his young wife Jane, his childhood sweetheart, whom he had married four years earlier when she was just sixteen. He looked at his son Jonathan age three, and his baby boy Moses, barely two months old. He didn't want to leave them, but Daniel and John should have been back months ago or at least somehow sent word.

The next day, as Jane choked back the tears, Squire Boone and his friend Alexander Neely disappeared down the same trail his brother had taken seven months earlier. Over two hundred miles away, to the northwest, and covering over one hundred thousand square miles, the area known as Kentucky was a hostile wilderness known only to Indians. Trying to find Daniel in such a vast, formidable territory, in the dead of winter, would be more difficult than looking for a needle in a haystack. But his love for his brother impelled him to try. Surely Daniel would do the same for him. It was a supreme test of brotherly love.

The trail, to the west and north, wound its tortuous course closer and closer to Kentucky as the days passed. On Squire pushed, over hills, past the headwaters of the Tennessee River, and through the pass in the mountains that would come to be known as the Cumberland Gap. Daniel Boone, himself, years later, recounted his experiences during those seven months beginning May 1, 1769*:

> After a long and fatiguing journey through a
> mountainous wilderness, in a westward direction,
> on the seventh day of June we found ourselves on

---

* Daniel dictated his adventures to John Filson, who no doubt embellished the language of the rough-hewn backwoodsman.

Red River. From the top of an eminence we saw with pleasure the beautiful level of Kentucky. For some time we had experienced the most uncomfortable weather, as a prelibation of our future sufferings.

At this place we encamped, made a shelter to defend us from the inclement season, and began to hunt and reconnoitre the country. We found everywhere an abundance of beasts of all sorts, through this vast forest. The buffalo were more frequent than I have seen cattle in the settlements, browsing on the leaves of cane, or cropping the herbage on those extensive plains. Sometimes we saw hundreds in a drove; and the numbers about the salt springs were amazing. Here we hunted with great success until the 22nd day of September.

Picture these half dozen pioneers dressed in deerskin shirt and trousers, coon-skin cap and moccasins, carrying powder horns, shot pouches, long rifles, knives, and tomahawks – Daniel Boone, John Finley, Joseph Holden, James Monay, William Cool, and John Stewart — after five weeks of toiling through the forest, and, finally, after a whole day of climbing the mountainside, beholding the fabled Red River Valley and the land of Kentucky. They reached the top of the mountain just at sunset, and as they came up to the point where they could survey the western landscape, a scene met their eyes surpassing their fondest dreams.

There before them lay the beautiful Kentucky River, fed by its many branches. They looked down upon broad plains, green slopes, and wooded dells. As far as their eyes could see, a seemingly endless prairie stretched, where countless herds of deer and buffalo roamed knowing no fear of man's encroachment. They marveled at the hundreds of wild turkeys; the thousands of pigeons; the woodchucks and squirrels in every tree; berries, fruits, nuts, clover, blue grass

Artist: Jack K. Hodgkin

Daniel Boone at Pilot Knob. On June 7, 1769, Daniel and his companions climbed Pilot Knob, and "from the top of an eminence we saw with pleasure the beautiful level of Kentucky."

– it was more than they had dared to dream. The setting sun tinted the land's breathtaking splendor with its golden rays as the six weary adventurers gazed awe-stricken at the beauty they beheld. The Canaan of all their hopes had been reached!

Here, on the top of the mountain, they built a crude shelter from boughs of trees, laced with strips of bark, for shelter from the summer rain. Day after day, during that summer of 1769, they hunted, then returned to camp each evening. They killed deer and buffalo and trapped and fished to their hearts' content. There was no hint of any danger, and as the summer progressed they became accustomed to the new life and relaxed their vigilance. But there was unseen danger lurking in this wilderness.

Unaware of what was about to happen, they began to plan their return to the Yadkin Valley. With their horses laden with the furs and pelts from a summer of successful hunting and trapping in this pristine wilderness, they started home, but they were planning to return the following year with their families to begin a new settlement.

Unfortunately, lowering their guard against the red men proved to be their undoing. Of the six pioneers, only Daniel Boone would live to see the Yadkin Valley again. They divided up, with Daniel and his brother-in-law going one way, and the other four exploring in a different direction. Daniel continued his story:

> On September 22nd, John (Stewart) and I had a pleasing ramble; but fortune changed the scene in the close of it. We had passed through a great forest, on which stood myriads of trees, some gay with blossoms, others rich with fruits. Nature was a series of wonders, and a fund of delight. Here she displayed her ingenuity and industry in a variety of flowers and fruits, beautifully colored, elegantly shaped, and charmingly flavored. We were diverted with innumerable animals presenting themselves perpetually to our view.
>
> In the decline of the day, near the Kentucky River, as we ascended the brow of a small hill, a number of Indians rushed out of a thick canebreak upon us, and made us prisoners. The time of our sorrow was now arrived, and the scene fully opened. The Indians plundered us of what we had, and kept us in confinement, treating us with common usage.

The Indians surprised them, and they were carried off as prisoners – a new experience for the man who was destined to become a legend. Confinement was a lifestyle Daniel Boone could not abide, and from the onset he plotted his escape.

Without weapons and outnumbered, Daniel and John would have to trick the Indians. To do this, they immediately agreed to show no sign of resistance to their captivity nor any desire of escape. Instead, they became docile captives – model prisoners. At the end of seven days of pretense, Daniel sensed that it was time to move. He continued the story:

> While we were prisoners we displayed no uneasiness nor demonstrated any desire to escape, which made them less suspicious of us. But in the dead of night, as we lay in thick canebreak by a large fire, when sleep had locked up their senses, my situation not disposing me for rest, I touched John and gently awoke him. We improved this favorable opportunity and departed, leaving them to take their rest.

Discovery of any attempted escape meant certain death. After midnight Daniel raised his head and looked around. His captors' deep breathing assured him that they were deeply asleep. They hadn't bothered to post a guard. Daniel gently awaked John, and they crept out of the camp, attempting to conceal their tracks as best they could.

By morning they had reached their own camp, only to find the others gone. Although their shelter had been broken up and plundered, giving evidence of violence, Daniel and John assumed that Finley, Holden, Monay, and Cool had broken camp themselves and had started for home and that their camp had been ransacked by the Indians after they had left. But their true fate will never be known; none of them was ever heard from again.

Now, Daniel and John were alone in the wilderness. Again they build a hut for protection – this time from the winds and snows of winter. Why they didn't start back to the Yadkin Valley is unknown. Perhaps they meant to replenish

Drawing by Andrew Filmer

Daniel Boone and John Stewart were both prisoners of the Indians. "I touched John and gently awoke him. We improved this favorable opportunity and departed, leaving them (the Indians) to take their rest."

the furs and pelts the Indians had stolen. But without horses, weapons, or supplies of any kind, the two trudged along on foot through the uncharted territory, next to the rushing waters of Station Camp Creek, a tributary of the Kentucky River. As they grew weak and dispaired of ever reaching their families, they spied two horsemen in the distance. Too exhausted to run, and without rifles, they were at the mercy of the approaching riders.

Nearer and nearer they came, as Daniel and John reconciled themselves to being recaptured. But as the riders grew closer, there was something about one of them that seemed vaguely familiar. Could it be? Or, was he dreaming? Daniel was too weak to shout, but he waved his arms. The riders, seeing the figures of two men struggling along the creek bank, rode quickly to investigate who the strangers dressed in buckskins might be.

Squire, suddenly recognizing the men, felt his heart leap for joy. He hurriedly dismounted, flung himself at Daniel, and they embraced in a rib-crunching hug. Incredible as it seems, Squire Boone had found his brother!

On March 2, 1942, Dr. Willard Rouse Jillson, in an address before the Filson Club of Louisville, Kentucky, said, "Many deeds of bravery and heroism mark the pages of early Kentucky history, but none can compare with this spontaneous, intelligent, and perfectly timed expedition designed and executed by Squire Boone to bring relief to his brother Daniel."

Daniel afterward declared that his younger brother Squire had become "an instrument ordained by Providence."

CHAPTER TWO

THE BROTHERS MEET AGAIN

The father of Daniel and Squire Boone was Squire Boone, Sr., whose home was in Berks County, Pennsylvania, near the present city of Reading. The senior Squire Boone was born in 1696, in Devonshire England, as were three generations of Boones before him.

When Squire Boone, Sr., was seventeen years of age, he migrated across the Atlantic to Philadelphia. At age twenty-four he was living in Berks County, Pennsylvania, and was married to Sarah Morgan. Squire, Sr. and Sarah were to become the parents of eleven children, all born near Reading. Daniel, born in 1734, was child number six, and Squire, Jr., born ten years later, was the tenth. The youngest was Hannah, whose husband was killed by Indians on the ill-fated expedition to Kentucky, leaving her a widow at age twenty-three.

Times were not easy for the Boones, and the hardships of raising a large family off the clearings of the forests were ever present. In 1747 they pulled up stakes and migrated to the Shenandoah Valley of Virginia near Winchester. Squire (Jr.) was three years old. Evidently life in Virginia did not improve the Boones' lot, and two years later they moved again – this time to North Carolina.

The east side of the South Yadkin River near the present city of Wilkesboro became their new home. Here, in

Photograph Courtesy of the Pennsylvania Historical and Museum Commission.
Squire Boone was born in this house near Reading, Pennsylvania in 1744. His family moved away when he was three years old. His brother Daniel was born and raised in this house also.

the foothills of the Smoky Mountains, Squire spent the carefree days of his boyhood, living the life of a lad on the frontier, his home a log cabin, and his playground the uncut forest which stretched endlessly in every direction.

With his older brother to teach him, he became an expert marksman with the gun of the frontier – the long rifle. When he was fifteen years of age, his mother took him with her on a return visit to Pennsylvania to see relatives. Squire's keen interest in guns brought an offer from his cousin, Samuel Boone, to learn the trade of gunsmithing. Squire, with his mother's blessing, remained in Pennsylvania with Samuel as a gunsmith's apprentice.

For nearly five years Squire worked diligently to make the finest rifles to be found. It was Squire who crafted Daniel Boone's famous "Tick Licker" rifle, which he presented to his brother as a gift. But four-and-a-half years of confinement in a gunshop were all Squire could stand. He longed for the

Photograph by Fr. Ralph W. Beiting

The Yadkin River in North Carolina where the Boone family relocated.

Photograph by Fr. Ralph W. Beiting

A replica of the Boone homestead along the Yadkin River where Squire lived. It is located in the Daniel Boone State Park southeast of Mocksville, North Carolina.

forest and the freedom of his youth in North Carolina. His parents, acceding to his wishes, purchased the remaining six months of his five year apprenticeship, and Squire returned to the land he had learned to love.

Now twenty years of age and back in North Carolina, Squire found still another love – fifteen-year-old Jane VanCleve, whom he had admired since she was a child. The following year Squire and Jane were married. For the first few months of their marriage, while Squire was building a log cabin for them between Bear Creek and the Yadkin River, Squire and Jane lived in a cave overlooking the Yadkin River. Caves featured prominently not only in Squire's life, but also in his death.

Though ten years separated their ages, Squire and Daniel were almost inseparable. They both had wanderlust, and when one of them felt the urge to explore, the other usually came along. Their first major trip together was in 1765, when Daniel was thirty-one, and Squire was twenty-one. Squire's new bride was left behind, an often repeated experience for the wife of an explorer and hunter. The brothers and three other men from the valley headed south to Florida.

There they explored the Altamaha River country, looking for a new and better place for a settlement. But when they found the region wet, covered with briars, and with little game, they returned home, eliminating Florida as a potential homesite. Yet, Squire, always a wanderer, did return to Florida a quarter of a century later.

This next journey followed two years after their return from Florida – in 1767, when Squire and Daniel headed northwest on a long hunting trip. Not realizing that they had travelled all the way to a land they would seek on their third

"TICK-LICKER"

*Daniel Boone's famous "Tick-Licker" rifle was made by Squire
Boone, a skilled gunsmith, who presented it to his brother as a
gift. The other side of the stock reads, "Boons Best Fren."*

trip, they spent the winter near what is now Prestonburg, Kentucky, and returned to the Yadkin Valley in the spring with all of the pelts their horses could carry. They were now thoroughly seasoned woodsmen, trappers, and trackers, and their wives were getting used to their being gone for months at a time.

During the following winter, they remained in the valley and became engrossed in the tales and legends told by an itinerant horse trader and peddler named John Finley. Daniel had known him in previous years and avidly listened as Finley told of the land of Kentucky with thick cane, meadowlands, and animals without number. Their imagination fired by Finley's stories, Daniel and Squire asked him if he would lead them there. Finley knew the way to the head of the Tennessee River where one passed on through the great gap in the mountains into this hunter's paradise. Finley readily agreed to lead a party of pioneers to the legendary land of Kentucky.

It was this party that left on the fateful spring morning of May first, 1769, beginning the adventure from which only Daniel Boone would return. Squire resisted the temptation to accompany them. Perhaps it was because his son, Moses, was just two months old. But for whatever reason, Squire stayed behind.

The group of well-wishers who had gathered to see them off – the Boones, VanCleves, Bryans, and others – possibly the Lincolns* – laughed and joked about the adventures the explorers would have when they found Kentucky. But Daniel's wife Rebecca and John Stewart's wife Hannah could not hold back the tears. Nor did Squire join in their

---

*Their neighbor and friend was John Lincoln, great-grandfather of Abraham Lincoln. One of Squire's cousins married John Lincoln's sister.

laughter. Somehow he felt this sojourn into Kentucky would have sobering consequences.

The scene that took place when Squire found Daniel along Station Camp Creek can be only imagined. Squire and Alex brought news from home – of the wives, families, and friends. Such a time of rejoicing it must have been! But it was all too short. John Stewart, fired with homesickness by Squire's news from the Yadkin Valley, was ready to return, even without furs or pelts, and who could blame him? His young wife Hannah (Squire and Daniel's sister) needed him. He had been away too long. When Daniel and Squire made the decision to stay on in Kentucky until spring, still determined not to return without pelts, John Stewart set off for home, accompanied by Alex Neely, who had arrived with Squire. Alex had no desire to spent the winter in Kentucky either.

Squire and Daniel had no way of knowing that Finley, Holden, Monay, and Cool had perished. Nor did they learn for several more months that John and Alex had failed to make it back to the Yadkin Valley and that their little sister, twenty-two-year old Hannah Boone Stewart was now a young widow. Of the eight men – six in the original party and two in the search party – only two survived – the brothers Daniel and Squire Boone.

It was the dead of winter, but the brothers determined to continue hunting and trapping, to elude the Indians, and to return home in the spring. They roamed magnificent forests and visited many choice spots, including the broad bottom of the Kentucky River near the mouth of Otter Creek, where in later years they would erect Fort Boonesborough.

In the courthouse lobby in Richmond, Kentucky, encased in glass, stands a huge stone slab found in southern

Madison County which reads, "1770 SQUIRE BOONE." The year of 1770 turned out to be not only the most eventful year for the Boone family, but probably the most eventful year in the founding of Kentucky.

The hunting was successful, and no Indians appeared. But when early spring turned into May, and it was time to return, Daniel had a change of heart. Although he had been gone from his home and family for an entire year and had finally replenished his supply of skins, he found the lure of his new-found paradise too much to overcome. It was stronger than the call of home.

Squire did not share Daniel's feelings. He had done his duty and located his lost brother. His love for his wife Jane and his two little boys, Jonathan and Moses, were strong enough to lure him back, but only after he had made a pact with Daniel to return. Laden with the pelts he and Daniel had acquired during the long winter, Squire set out by himself for North Carolina. Determined to stay on in Kentucky, even though alone, Daniel Boone waved goodbye as Squire disappeared over the ridge.

The brothers had agreed on a plan before parting. Squire was to explain to Daniel's wife Rebecca that they were preparing the way for a new settlement in the land of plenty. Squire promised to return with horses, guns, and provisions. In the vast wilderness of Kentucky, they chose the exact spot where they would meet: at Daniel's old shelter on Station Camp Creek near the spot Squire had first found him. Not only did they choose the place; they chose the exact time – at noon on July 27, 1770.

Heading for home, Squire made good time and got all the way to the east side of the Cumberland Mountains when his fears were realized. Now it was *his* turn to be captured by Indians. They surprised him, robbing him of most of the pelts and furs he and Daniel had taken during the winter. Luckily, the Indians wanted only his possessions and not his life. They traded him a worthless Indian rifle for his good one, took his horse, rode away, and left him standing in the trail. He walked the rest of the way home to North Carolina.

It was a momentous day in the Yadkin Valley when Squire walked into view. His young wife Jane and their two boys gave him a joyous welcome. Daniel's wife and family received the news with glad hearts that their husband and father was alive, well, and determined to begin a new settlement in Kentucky. But for Hannah Boone and the wives, children, and friends of the others – John Finley, Joseph Holden, James Monay, William Cool, John Stewart, and Alexander Neely, the news was grim. They had set out for home many months ago. Now little hope was left that they were still alive.

Squire stayed in the Yadkin Valley only long enough to trade for new horses, powder, bullets, and a few supplies the few pelts that had survived the Indians' raid. We can only guess Jane Boone's reaction to her husband's plans for returning quickly to Kentucky.

The brothers Squire and Daniel Boone were driven by wanderlust and pioneering instincts we may find difficult to comprehend today, but it was these instincts that moved America's frontier westward.

On his round trip Squire had covered over seven hundred miles. Now he was determined to make the return trip to a specific forest clearing over three hundred miles away – and to arrive at noon on July the twenty-seventh. As Jane wept, and the two boys hung to his neck, Squire broke away and disappeared down the same trail into the forest he had taken more than a year previously. At that time, he had been searching for Daniel and had found him. Now he had a

The *"Squire Boone Rock"* is encased in glass in the lobby of the courthouse at Richmond, Kentucky.

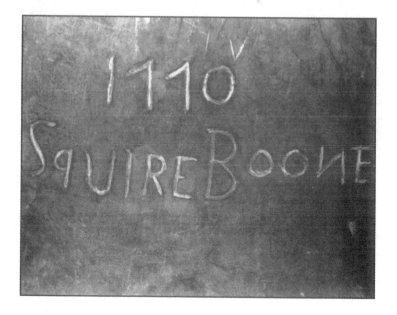

Squire Boone Rock

Daniel Boone's brother, Squire Boone carved this stone after returning to Madison County, Kentucky from Virginia. It is legend that the simple inscription, "1770 - Squire Boone" was carved by the pioneer to inform his brother that he was in the vicinity again.

Found in the southern part of the county between Big Hill and Pilot Knob, it was presented to Madison County officials by J. Len Ballard on October 7, 1892.

The obelisk-shaped stone was displayed on the courthouse lawn until 1965.

Squire (a birth name, not a title) was a Calvinistic Baptist preacher and performed the state's first marriage ceremony at Boonesborough in 1776.

SITE OF FORT BOONESBOROUGH

Squire and Daniel discovered the future site of Fort Boonesborough in 1770.

Another view of the site from the opposite bank of the Kentucky River.

second appointment with Daniel, and he meant to keep it.

The exact date Squire started down the trail has been lost to history, but it was most likely during the third or fourth week of June 1770. Although no record has survived of Squire's second sojourn into Kentucky, years later Daniel recounted to his biographer, John Filson, the story of the three months he himself spent alone in the wilderness waiting for Squire's return:

> Alone, by myself, without bread, salt, or sugar, without the company of any fellow creature – even a horse or dog, I confess I never before was under greater necessity of exercising philosophy and fortitude. A few days I passed comfortably. The idea of a beloved wife and family, and their anxiety upon the account of my absence and exposed situation, made sensible impressions upon my heart. A thousand dreadful apprehensions presented themselves to my view, and had undoubtedly disposed me to melancholy if further indulged.

Daniel, obviously homesick, dreamed of Rebecca and the children. He still had no idea that six of his companions, including his sister's husband were dead. And he surely must have wondered constantly if Squire had made it back home and if he would safely return to keep their appointed meeting. But Daniel kept busy. He continued his story:

> One day I undertook a tour through the country, and the diversity and beauties of nature I met with in this charming season expelled every gloomy and vexatious thought. Just at the close of day the gentle gales retired, and left the place to the disposal of a profound calm. Not a breeze shook the most tremulous leaf. I had gained the summit of a commanding ridge, and looked around with astonishing delight to behold ample plains and beauteous tracts below. On the other hand I

surveyed the famous Ohio River, that rolled in silent dignity, marking the western boundary of Kentucky with inconceivable grandeur.

At a vast distance I beheld the mountains lift their venerable brows and penetrate the clouds. All things were still. I kindled a fire near a fountain of sweet water and feasted on the loin of a buck which a few hours before I had killed.

Daniel had gone a considerable distance from his camp, exploring all the way to the Ohio River. It was time for him to make his way back to Station Camp Creek to meet Squire. He had the utmost faith in his younger brother. Daniel resumed his story:

I continued this tour, and in a few days explored a considerable part of the country, each day equally pleased as the first. I returned to my old camp, which was not disturbed in my absence. I did not confine my lodging to it, but often reposed in the thick canebreaks to avoid the savages, who I believe often visited my camp, but fortunately for me, in my absence. In this situation I was constantly exposed to danger and death.

How did Daniel keep track of the days? Did he make himself a crude calendar on which he marked off each day as he bedded down for the night? Or did he carry a stick which he notched each day? And what of Squire? He had to keep track of the days also. Whatever method they used worked well.

July the twenty-seventh found Daniel hiding in the canebreak next to his camp. The sun was now directly overhead. Although Daniel's heart must have been beating faster than usual, his keen ears heard a twig snap. Then as he watched in both amazement and profound relief, Squire stepped into the clearing at exactly twelve noon!

CHAPTER THREE

"YOU CAN MARRY US"

After a trip alone through seven hundred miles or more of uncharted wilderness and unknown trails, to arrive at an appointed time and place is miraculous. Many times over the years, Daniel himself told of Squire's accomplishment of this feat. Squire had brought with him provisions and a pair of horses; and the brothers spent the rest of the summer and all of the fall and winter exploring the rivers and valleys of southeastern Kentucky between the Green and Cumberland Rivers, to which they gave names.

Although they found much evidence of Indians, they were able to avoid them. An early Boone biography by George Canning Hill, published in 1859, states: "For eight months these two men roamed over the tract of territory upon which they had entered, and were not once molested. It is the strangest of all facts recorded in the history of settlements, and goes to show that the Boones had, in reality, hit upon their true destiny as pioneers."

For the first time Daniel learned that none of the others had survived. Squire delivered all the news from home, including the fact that the pioneers in the Yadkin Valley were murmuring about foreign rule, which they felt was oppressing. The story of the Boston Massacre had sent a chill of horror through the valley.

With the two horses Squire had brought, they made good time back to North Carolina, unmolested by the Indians. Their families and friends received them with delight and wonder. Squire and Daniel had many exciting adventures to relate of life in the wilderness and of the many dangers they had passed through safely. Their listeners were filled with fear, but their imaginations were fired with the stories of incomparable scenery – mountains, valleys, plains, rivers – and game abundant beyond belief.

One physical feature they described was the prevalence of large depressions in the limestone soil between the Green and Cumberland Rivers, which they termed "sinkholes." It was in the area of these sinkholes that the brothers determined one day to establish a permanent settlement. This was the finest part of all the land they had explored, and here they decided to bring their families to begin a new life.

Perhaps Squire and Daniel did not yet realize that these sinkholes were the evidence of collapsed passageways and chambers of caves and caverns beneath the earth's surface, which nature had carved out of the limestone over hundreds of thousands of years. Nor could they have suspected that some two decades later they would discover one of the most beautiful and spectacular caves in America – a cave with profuse formations and underground rivers and waterfalls – to which Squire would return as an old man to spend his final years, and then be buried within its majestic chambers.

It was April of 1771, when Squire and Daniel arrived back home, and they earnestly set about organizing a wagon train of Yadkin Valley pioneers to settle Kentucky. They wanted to leave as soon as possible, but it wasn't to be. They were the only two to live to return from Kentucky. Six others had perished. The pioneers were understandably afraid. Squire and Daniel sought the assistance of the English government since America was still an English colony. Independence was another three years away. But no help was made available. It was up to the Boone brothers themselves to organize the move over the mountains. But the forty men they mustered were not enough to fend off an Indian attack, and the wagon train was doomed.

On October 10, 1771, the wagons reached Powell's Valley. As they stopped to rest, seven of the men, including Daniel's seventeen year old son James left the group to round up some cattle which had strayed. Indians stealthily tracked them, and without warning the bloodthirsty savages butchered them. Only one of the six lived to tell what had happened.

The lone survivor of the attack was Adam, a negro slave who belonged to Col. Russell, one of the pioneers. Adam told how young James Boone and the others had been tortured. The Indians tore out their fingernails by the roots and cut the palms of their hands with long knives as the boys held up their hands to defend themselves. Adam heard James pleading with the Indians to end his life quickly, and they soon killed him.

Rebecca gave Daniel her best linen sheet to wrap their son's body for burial. They buried him and covered his grave with stones to protect it from wolves. Daniel and Rebecca, grief-stricken over the loss of their firstborn son, did not argue when the others voted to turn back. Once again Squire and Daniel returned to the Yadkin Valley, this time with all family members except James. To date, twelve of the Yadkin Valley pioneers had been killed by Indians on the way to or from Kentucky.

Yet, Squire and Daniel never gave up their dream of a new settlement. They bided their time. Several years passed. It was now March of 1775. Ten years of marriage to Jane had

DEATH OF BOONE'S SON

NEAR HERE, OCTOBER 10, 1773, JAMES BOONE, SON OF DANIEL BOONE, AND HENRY RUSSELL MEMBERS OF BOONE'S PARTY ON THE WAY TO KENTUCKY, WERE SURPRISED AND KILLED BY INDIANS.

Photograph by Father Ralph Beiting

In addition to James Boone and Henry Russell, five other young men were tortured and killed as well. The only one to escape this massacre was Adam, a Negro slave owned by Henry Russell's father, who lived to tell of the others' horrible fate.

brought Squire three boys and a girl. Jonathan was nine, Moses six, Isaiah one, and Sarah was a newborn baby. Squire's time was filled from daylight to dark providing food, clothing, and necessities for his growing family. Squire was a dependable husband and an exemplary father.

In the evening, as his children played on the cabin floor, and Jane busied herself with household tasks, Squire often read his Bible before the fire. He became conscious of the guiding Spirit of the Lord in his life, and kneeling on the hearth of his humble pioneer log cabin, he accepted salvation. In the days that followed he felt an inner urge to share the Word of God with his people, and he became an occasional preacher at gatherings of Calvanistic Baptists in the valley.

These pioneers came to love Squire for his simple and ardent faith in God. As an old man, nearly four decades later, he carved his enduring faith into the foundation stones of the gristmill he and his sons built:

I set and sing my soul's salvation and

Bless the God of my creation.

His carving onto the stones continued:

My God my life hath much befriended.

I'll praise Him til my days are ended.

Photograph by Mike Tonegawa
Squire Boone's original carvings in stone are on display in Boone's Mill at Squire Boone Village near Corydon, Indiana.

Artist: Russell May

Squire and Daniel Boone are depicted leading the settlers (far right) through the Cumberland Gap.

Now the ardent Christian, Squire Boone, with his brother Daniel and twenty-eight more men set about cutting out the "Wilderness Road" from Cumberland Gap to the mouth of Otter Creek in what is now Madison County Kentucky. On March the twenty-fifth, they were attacked by Indians near today's Richmond, Kentucky, south of Lexington. One of the men was killed, but Squire and Daniel were unhurt.

On April first, they arrived at the "plain on the South Side" of the Kentucky River at a salt lick, where Squire assisted in building the first log fort sixty yards from the river's edge, which they aptly named "Boonesborough." At Fort Boonesborough, on May 25, 1775, the first legislature of Kentucky met. Squire, acting as a delegate, introduced a bill "to preserve the range." Squire became the first environmentalist west of the Appalachians.

Nearly a half-century later, Squire's son Moses, a lad of six, helped to supervise construction of the capitol building for still another new state, Indiana.

Squire built a cabin not far from Fort Boonesborough on the bank of its tributary, Silver Creek. More settlers were now coming down the Ohio and Kentucky Rivers and through the Cumberland Gap looking for homesites. Many of them put down around Fort Boonesborough.

In early 1776, Squire sold his cabin and once again returned to the Yadkin Valley of North Carolina, this time to bring back Jane and the children for good. He also brought Daniel's family, as well as many others. They all stayed at the fort while cabins were being built and claims cut out on the trees in the nearby wilderness. But the Indians, who were afraid to attack the fort, found their chance on July the

Artist: Jack K. Hodgkin

At Kentucky's First Legislative Assembly, Squire Boone, a delegate, introduced a bill to "preserve the range," which made him Kentucky's first environmentalist.

Artist: Jack K. Hodgkin

Three teenage girls living at Fort Boonesborough – 16 year old Betsey Calloway; her sister, 14 year old Fanny Calloway; and Daniel Boone's 14 year old daughter Jemima were captured by Indians as they crossed the Kentucky River in a canoe.

The girls are rescued. Daniel and Squire Boone, Col. Calloway, and several others tracked the Indians over 40 miles, surprised them, and retrieved the frightened girls. All three of the girls were married within several months.

At the extreme right of the picture, on the opposite shore, is the spot where the three teenage girls were abducted by the Indians on July 14, 1776. The location was designated as "The Four Sycamores."

fourteenth when three teenage girls carelessly left the fort and crossed the Kentucky River.

For a lark sixteen-year-old Elizabeth ("Betsey") and fourteen-year-old Frances ("Fanny") Calloway, along with Daniel's fourteen-year-old daughter Jemima Boone, paddled a canoe across the river. As they landed on the opposite shore, five Indians, who were lying in wait, pushed the now empty canoe out into the river, cutting off their escape; then they dragged the screaming girls into the forest.

As soon as the girls were missed, their fathers, Daniel Boone and Col. Calloway, organized a search party with Squire and five other men, who set out in pursuit. Betsey and Fanny's father later recounted the story:

> "Next morning by daylight we were on the track. We observed their course, and travelled upwards of 30 miles. We pursued and overtook them just as they were kindling a fire to cook. We discovered each other nearly at the same time. Four of us fired, and all rushed on them."

Daniel, Squire, Col. Calloway, and the five others had tracked the Indians for two days for some forty miles. They killed two of the Indians and "recovered the three little broken-hearted girls."

One evening about three weeks after the rescue, Squire heard a knock at his log cabin door. Answering, he was surprised to see Betsey Calloway, and with her a young man he immediately recognized as Samuel Henderson, the younger brother of Captain Henderson. He bade them enter his humble cabin.

"And what may I do for you?" Squire inquired of the young couple. With a twinkle in her eye, Betsey spoke up, "Elder Boone, sir, you can marry us."

Artist: Harold D. Collins

The building of Fort Boonesborough

Artist: Russell May

Fort Boonesborough completed as viewed from the opposite bank of the Kentucky River.

A sketch of Fort Boonesborough based on the original drawing by Captain Henderson.

CHAPTER FOUR

AT WAR WITH THE INDIANS

On August 7, 1776, the self-ordained Baptist minister, Elder Squire Boone, joined Elizabeth Calloway and Samuel Henderson in holy matrimony, which went on record as the first marriage ever performed west of the Appalachian Mountains. Betsey's wedding dress was made of white linen. Her mother's present to the new bride and groom was a mattress made from corn shucks. The new husband's gift to his bride was a cabin built by him inside the fort. It was the thirtieth cabin to be built inside the stockade walls. By the light of tallow "dips," the wedding was celebrated with fiddle music, dancing, and a meal of both wild and tame meat, vegetables, biscuits, blackberry cobbler, and watermelons.

Within several more months the other two girls, Fanny Calloway and Jemima Boone, though both were only fourteen years of age, were married. Although no records exist of who performed the marriages, we can assume it was Squire since he was Jemima's uncle, and he had performed the ceremony for Fanny's sister.

Introduction of the first environmental bill before the Kentucky Legislature, performance of the first marriage ceremony in Kentucky — what would Squire do next? He and Jane had another first on the way. She soon gave birth to their fifth and last child, Enoch, who became the first white child born in Kentucky.

The first marriage
west of the
Appalachians

An artist's conception of Squire Boone marrying Betsey Calloway and Samuel Henderson. Squire had helped rescue sixteen-year-old Betsey from Indians just four weeks earlier.

From the day the Indians kidnapped the young girls, they kept the fort under constant surveillance. They watched the incursion of the white man with jealousy, and they dreaded the protection that their fort offered them. But when the settlers left the fort they were in grave danger. A man could be out plowing, and a bullet from the rifle of a hidden Indian might go whizzing past his head. If cattle were left outside the compound overnight, they might be missing or dead the next morning. The winter of 1775-1776 was a long, gloomy ordeal fraught with constant fear of the savages. Still, the Indians were afraid to attack the fort.

Winter passed, and during the summer, Squire ventured to a spot in present Shelby County, Kentucky, some seventy miles from Boonesborough, which he had explored the previous year. He liked it there, and he planted a corn crop. With a pick he engraved a stone with his name and date, coloring his engraving with red paint he had fashioned. This marker indicated Squire's claim to the land, which came to be called "Painted Stone Station."

Twenty years later, Squire was called back to Painted Stone Station, now called "Boone's Station on Clear Creek" by the Shelby County Court, who required Squire to identify it in a deposition. Here are Squire's own words, as recorded by the court:

> In the summer in the year 1775, I, this deponant, came to the place where Boone's Station on Clear Creek was built. I then made a small improvement, about one quarter of a mile North of where the Old Mill at said Boones Station now stands. In the Spring of the year 1776, I came again to the same place, and took a stone out of the creek, and with a mill pick, picked my name, in full, and the date of the year thereon, and with red paint, I painted the letters and figures all red. From which stone this Tract of land took the name of "The Painted Stone" tract. The said stone was about one inch thick and eighteen inches long and wide. The place which I now show about one hundred yards above the said Old Mill, bank of the creek, is the place where I marked it as aforsaid and left it there until it was about three years afterward carried away by some person; and further saith not.

(signed) Squire Boone

Historian Willard R. Jillson states that during the active period of settlement from 1780 to 1790, Squire Boone's Painted Stone Station "was the only place of dependable refuge of the settlers in that great sweep of country between the forts at Harrodsburg on the south, Lexington on the east, and Louisville on the west." But in 1776, there were still not enough men to build and secure a fort at Painted Stone.

In 1775 a Captain Harrod had come down the Ohio

River, and with a band of followers had erected a "station" or fort in the area known today as Harrodsburg, Kentucky, a distance of some forty miles from Fort Boonesborough. In 1777, Squire with his family – Jane and their five children – moved from Fort Boonesborough to Fort Harrod.

One day, while Squire and two other men were harvesting their corn crop outside the fort, they were attacked by three Indians. One of Squire's companions was killed outright. Squire shot one of the Indians, and engaged the other two in hand-to-hand combat, killing one of them with his silver-hilted sword. The other ran in fear. But this Indian fight left Squire scared for life. A tomahawk wound to his forehead left a scar he carried to his grave.

Just two weeks after this Indian fight, Squire was shot in yet another encounter with an Indian and suffered a broken rib. Years later, in recalling the incident to one of his sons, he said, "That was the best little Indian fight I was ever in ... both parties stood and fought so well."

Settlers were beginning to spread out over Kentucky's meadows and valleys, and along the rivers and streams. They built scattered cabins and shelters, but many of the brave pioneers were killed by Indians. It became apparent that unless they could flee to the safety of a fort, when Indians were near, that there was no use in building a cabin or attempting a settlement.

In 1777 there were only one hundred and two men in three forts defending the frontier from the Indians: twenty-two men at Fort Boonesborough, fifteen at Fort Harrod and sixty-five at Logan's Fort. The two smaller forts had to be bolstered. Daniel had been captured by Indians and taken north, leaving Boonesborough in need of a leader. So, Squire answered the call. He and his family moved back to Fort

Boonesborough, and Squire led the effort to build stronger fortifications in preparation for a major Indian attack. It was well that Squire hastily strengthened the fort. Indian Chief Black Fish was busy making plans to wipe it out.

On August 8, 1778, Black Fish, with some four hundred and fifty warriors, along with several British soldiers who were friendly to the Indians, surrounded the fort. Black Fish and the British called for a council. The "forters" selected eight men to represent them, including Squire and Daniel, who had escaped and returned in time to be included. The others were Richard and Flanders Calloway,* William and Stephen Hancock, Major William Bailey Smith, and William Buchanan. They were to meet Indian and British representatives about sixty yards in front of the stockade gate. The

Artist: Major James Channon

In September, 1778, Blackfish, a Pawnee Chieftan, with 450 Indians and a dozen French-Canadian soldiers acting for the British, surrounded Fort Boonesborough.

---

*Flanders Calloway had married Daniel Boone's daughter Jemima.

Squire Boone, and the other Fort Boonesborough representatives at the peace treaty, which was merely a treacherous rouse by the Indians, rush back to the fort. Squire was shot and nearly died from his wound. Daniel cut the bullet out of Squire's shoulder, as Squire held a broadax in readiness in case the Indians got inside the fort. He determined to take at least one Indian with him in death.

purpose of the council was for the British to implore the settlers to surrender, avoiding slaughter.

Squire and Daniel suggested at the council that they be given forty-eight hours to think it over, but surrender never really entered their minds. They wanted time to get as many of their cows and horses inside the stockade as possible, as well as time to carry in as much water as they could. While the men rounded up the animals, the women and children carried water. During this forty-eight-hour period of truce, the Indians merely watched and waited.

At the end of the allotted time the Indians made an arbor of tree limbs, and the women of the fort carried out refreshments for the negotiators as they discussed terms of a compromise. The settlers proposed that the Indians withdraw and that the forters abandon the fort. In truth, however, the forters had no intention of abandoning the fort, nor did the Indians have any intention of withdrawing.

The Indians pretended to accept the offer as they lit and passed around the traditional peacepipe. Each representative from both sides stood, shook hands, and took a puff from the pipe to seal the arrangement. The final puff on the peacepipe was the prearranged signal for the Indians to attack. Immediately, two Indian warriors sprang onto the backs of each of the eight forters, but the forters anticipated the Indians' treachery and were ready.

The remaining men in the fort had their rifles aimed at the Indians, and they began to pick them off. While the marksmen mowed down Indian after Indian, the eight forters in the peace ceremony struggled to get free. An eyewitness from atop the walk of the fort said, "Squire threw Indians from his back like so many little children." Not only did Squire save himself; he freed several of the others. He was then the last man to run toward the safety of the fort.

Before he could make it to the gate, an Indian rifle ball brought him down. Yet he managed to get up and dash the rest of the way, only to find that the stockade door had already been barred from within. Undismayed, he ran around the fort and literally dove through a secret door, disguised as part of the wall, which he himself had designed.

According to Squire Boone historian Ted L. Igleheart, "This incredible feat of agility while wounded, unselfishness, and courage, remain unmatched except by Squire Boone himself in both previous and yet-to-come adventures. Only the escape from captivity of his brother Daniel are comparable, but none were matched by the overall prowess of Squire."

CHAPTER FIVE

SIMON GIRTY VS. SQUIRE BOONE

What has gone down in American pioneer history as "The Siege of Fort Boonesborough" had just begun. Inside the fort, sixty-five men, along with the women and children, wondered if they could withstand and prevail against some four hundred and fifty Indians who had them surrounded. They had food and water. Their greatest fears hinged on their scant supply of ammunition and the threat of fire. They knew, as did the Indians, that their fort was combustible.

To increase their supply of ammunition, Squire, though painfully injured, directed them to pick up rifle balls off the ground, and even to pick them out of the log walls of the fort. The forters fired at the Indians only when they had a good shot lined up, with an Indian in their rifle sights. Their aim was good. From his bed of pain, Squire gave instructions for the building of two types of devices which were to have a profound effect in saving the fort.

First, he used his ingenuity to bind black gum logs with an old wagon's metal tires, making them resemble cannons. Two imitation cannons were constructed to Squire's specifications and exposed to the Indians' view. But Squire wasn't through. Gunpowder charges with twenty-ounce rifle balls were actually detonated. The balls from the makeshift cannons landed near the Indians. The "cannons" finally burst from use, but not before they had frightened the Indians, who kept their distance.

Next, Squire gave instructions for the building of what must have been the first fire extinguishers in Kentucky. Buckets of water would not only expend the precious fluid they would need to survive, but in throwing the water up onto the roofs of the fort they would be exposed to arrows and bullets. Squire, realizing that the Indians would likely attempt to set the fort on fire with flaming arrows, came up with a novel plan to extinguish roof fires. Old rifle barrels were salvaged, wooden pistons made to fit inside the barrels, and the women and children were pressed into service as firefighters to squirt water up onto the roofs while they were in the fort below, safe from the arrows and bullets.

The Indians did shoot flaming arrows, and Squire's extinguishers worked like a charm, putting out the fires as fast as the burning arrows landed.

The Indians, thwarted with their arrows and bullets, attempted to tunnel under the stockade walls. But the forters cut a trench across their tunnel, and the sharpshooters picked them off one by one. A lull in the fighting gave Squire a chance to rest and gather enough strength to permit the removal of the lead in his shoulder. There was only one person in the fort that he trusted to remove the bullet. His brother Daniel cut open the wound with his hunting knife and took out the bullet. As Squire lay on his cot recovering, he kept a broadax next to his good arm. He later explained that it was for use "in the event of the last action." By this Squire meant that, if the Indians stormed the fort and got inside, he would take at least one of them with him in death.

But after ten days of siege, the Indians gave up hope of capturing or annihilating the defenders of Fort Boonesborough. Thirty-seven of the warriors had been killed by the forters' bullets. They finally drifted away into the forest, dejected and defeated, and the forters were able to open the gates to their hard-won freedom. Only two had been killed, and four, including Squire, Daniel, and Jemima, wounded. It took months for Squire to completely recover from his wound. The bullet had shattered the upper bone of his arm, which did not mend properly. That arm always remained shorter than the other. But scarred, and somewhat disfigured, Squire had lost none of his verve as a formidable defender of the frontier.

By the time another year had rolled around, Squire, in 1799, moved Jane and the children back to Fort Harrod. During the move they were shot at by Indians, and a man they had hired to help carry their household goods was killed, but the family made it safely into the fort. Squire, always the roamer, kept his family at Ford Harrod for only several months. Then loading their belongings onto a boat, he cast off into the Kentucky River traveling on down the Ohio River toward a new destination – a village called Louisville at the falls of the Ohio River, which had been named for the king of France. A land court had been set up there to record claims, and on November 22, 1779, Squire took title to several thousand acres, including the land back at Painted Stone on Clear Creek, which he had laid claim to previously. The court records state:

"Squire Boone this day claimed a settlement and preemption to a tract of Land lying on Silver Creek known by the name of Stockfields a branch of the Kentucky, by improving the same and raising a crop of Corn in the year 1776 and residing in the Country ever since. Satisfactory proof being made to the Court they are of Opinion that the said Boone has a right to a settlement of 400 Acres of Land to include the said improvement and the preemption of 1000 adjoining and that a certificate issue accordingly."

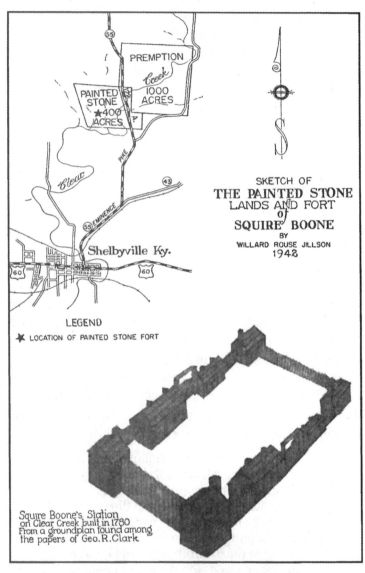

Sketch of THE PAINTED STONE, lands and fort, of Squire Boone, north of Shelbyville, Kentucky. Squire Boone's Station built in 1780, was on Clear Creek.

Later, on the same day, Squire Boone caused another certificate to be issued by the Court "for and in behalf of Benjamin VanCleve," his brother-in-law, to a settlement of 400 acres and an adjoining preemption of 1000 acres on Clear Creek known as the "Painted Stone."

> "Squire Boone for and in behalf of Benjamin VanCleve this day claimed a settlement and pre-emption to a tract of Land lying on Clear Creek known by the name of the Painted Stone a branch of Brashiers Creek a branch of Salt River by the said VanCleve's improving the same and raising a Crop of Corn in the year 1776. Satisfactory proof being made to the Court they are of Opinion that the said VanCleve has a right to a settlement of 400 Acres of Land including the said Improvement and the preemption of 1000 Acres of Land adjoining and that a Certificate issue accordingly."*

Squire divided his time between Painted Stone, where he began the construction of a new fort, and Louisville, where he bought land on high ground near the mouth of Bear Grass Creek, on which he built a cabin to spend the winter. As a resident of Louisville, he signed the early petitions of 1779 and 1780, which were presented to the Virginia Legislature in Richmond (Virginia) for formal chartering to the village at the falls. That winter Squire performed another of his "firsts."

As a Baptist minister he delivered the first church sermon in the fledgling village of Louisville, which was destined to become the largest city in Kentucky, a thriving metropolis and home to one of the largest Baptist Seminaries in the United States.

---

*From the Certificate Book of the Virginia Land Commission, *The Register* of the Kentucky State Historical Society, Volume 21, January, 1923, pages 55, 56

After spending the winter in Louisville, in the spring of 1780, Squire moved his family back to Painted Stone, where he began to build a "station" or fort on Clear Creek. Today, Shelbyville, Kentucky, is just 2 1/2 miles south of Painted Stone. Squire, in a letter dated June 28, 1780, to Col. Bowman, listed the names of the twenty-three Indian fighters at Painted Stone of which he was Captain:

Painted Stone, Ky.

June 28, 1780.

To Col. Bowman:

Sir:

I have sent you a list of our strength. I know not if it is necessary to Right down their names. Nevertheless being little trouble I have done it. Our strength is 23 men, to-wit:

Squire Boone, Captain	John McFadden
Alex Bryant	John Nichols
John Buckler	Peter Raul
Richard Cates	John Stapleton
Charles Doelman	Robert Tyler
John Eastwood	Abraham Van Meter
Joseph Eastwood	Allen Wickersham
Jeremiah Harris	Jacob Wickersham
Abraham Holt	Peter Wickersham
Morgan Hughes	James Wright
Evan Hinton	George Yunt

Squire Boone

While living at Painted Stone in 1780 and 81, Squire served as a Justice Of The Peace in Jefferson County, and performed marriage ceremonies for many couples. During this time he again had his property surveyed. The records in the original land office at Frankfort read as follows:

"Surveyed for Mr. Squire Boone assee. of Benjamin Vanclieve, by virtue of a Certificate from the Commissioners for right of Settlement 400 acres of Land lying on Clear Creek a fork of Brashears Creek called "The Painted Stone." John Stapleton and Philip Nicolas Chainmen Squire Boone Marker. March 8th, 1781.

"Beginning at a large white oak Buckeye and Hickory marked So B on the West side of Clear Creek Extending thence S 21 E 270 poles to B a Honey locust small Walnut Wht. Thorn Ironwood and small Hickory marked S B (at 120 poles X the Creek) thence W 263 poles to C two sugar-trees a Mulberry and Hickory marked S B (at 20 po. X the Creek at 106 x the Creek again) thence N 21 W 270 to D two small sugartrees and a Mulberry marked So B (at 28 poles X the Creek) thence E 253 poles to the beginning.

William Peyton, Asst.
Geo. May, S J c

Jefferson County
Variation 3° East

"Surveyed for Mr. Squire Boone, by virtue of a Preemption Warrant 1000 acres of Land on both sides of Clear Creek a fork of Brashears Creek adjoining his Settlement called 'The Painted Stone Tract.' John Stapleton and Robt. Tyler, Chainmen Squire Boone, Marker.

"Beginning at a large white oak buckeye and Hickory marked So B corner of the Settlement Extending thence E 99 poles to an Elm Ironwood Hickory and white oak marked So B on the side of a hill near the Creek, thence S 153 po. (X the Creek at 7 po. again at 64 po. and again at 100) to a Hickory Elm and Ironwood marked S B thence E 331 poles to two white ash and Sugartree marked S. B thence N 408 poles (at 310 X the Creek again at 404 po.) to a white oak and buckeye marked So B on the East side of the Creek, thence W 430 po. (x the Creek at 6 po.) to a sugartree and ask & white oak marked So B, thence South 255 poles to the Beginning.

March 8, 1781
Variation 3° East   William Peyton, Asst.
                                                    Geo. May, S J C

"Surveyed for Mr. Squire Boone by virtue of a Treasury Warrant 122 acres of Land on both sides of Clear Creek adjoining his Settlement and preemption called 'The Painted Stone Tract.' John Stapleton & Asam Wickersham Chainman, Squire Boone Marker. July 8, 1781.

"Beginning at a Honey locust small walnut and white Thorn Ironwood and small hickory marked So B corner to his Settlement, Extending thence E 67 poles to a Hoopwood and Sugar Tree growing from one root and two buckeye marked So B thence N 100 poles to a Honey locust Walnut and Buckeye marked So B in the line of his preemption thence with the said line W 67 poles to a Hickory Elm and Ironwood marked So B corner to the preemption thence with another of the said lines N 153 poles to an Elm Ironwood Hickory and White oak marked So B another of the said corners thence with another of the said lines W 99 poles to a large white oak buckeye and Hickory marked So B corner to the Settlement thence S 21 E° 270 poles to the Beginning.

Will Peyton Asst.
Geo May S. F. C.

Variation 3° E
Jefferson County

SIMON GIRTY VS. SQUIRE BOONE

In 1781 the fort was attacked by Indians. It was a surprise attack, and Squire was caught wearing only a white shirt. Several of the forters were killed, and Squire was gravely wounded. One bullet entered his right arm and another entered his right side. These wounds were so serious that it was thought for a time that he might not survive, but the indominable Squire pulled through. His arm had been shattered, and it remained one-and-one-half inches shorter than his left arm for the rest of his life.

Simon Girty, the infamous white renegade who was often referred to as the "White Indian," had led the Indians in the attack on Painted Stone, and he often laughed and boasted about how he had made "Squire Boone's shirttail fly." Indian attacks on the fort continued, so the fort was abandoned. On September 17, 1781, Squire, still an invalid from the attack, returned with his family to Louisville.

The year following, 1782, Squire, though still suffering greatly from the shoulder wound he had received at Boonesborough, as well as from the more recent wounds at Painted Stone, was elected and served as a representative of Jefferson County, Virginia, (Kentucky was not yet a state and was considered part of Virginia) in the House of Delegates in Richmond, Virginia, from May to December. While he was in Richmond, he moved his family back to Fort Harrod for safety.

With his unhealed wounds, his backwoods manner, and dressed in the frontiersman garb of doeskin and leather, Squire made eloquent and touching appeals before the Legislature on behalf of the settlers on the frontier. Throughout the rest of his life he recalled with pleasure the warm and sincere reception afforded him by his fellow legislators, all of whom were dressed in finery. His appeals for relief for the settlers in the west easily won the legislators' hearts and their approval.

Simon Girty, the renegade "White Savage", liked to boast that he made Squire Boone's shirttail fly. In an Indian raid he orchestrated against Squire Boone's Painted Stone Fort in 1781, he shot Squire, who almost died from the wounds and, who was more than a year in fully recovering.

During the winter of 1782-83, Squire and his family lived near Fort Harrod. In the fall, he journeyed to eastern Virginia and brought back his cousin, Samuel, to whom he had been apprenticed as a gunsmith a quarter of a century before. In 1784-85, Squire rebuilt Painted Stone, which had been burned to the ground by the Indians. He added a gristmill and a sawmill at the fort, and set about accumulating land. He made entry for over 58,000 acres of Bluegrass farmland through a scheme he devised. His method was to enter land claims for wealthy Virginians, execute surveys with clear titles, and give them half of the land, while keeping title to the other half for himself. In this way he became the largest landowner in what is now Shelby County, Kentucky.

He became a member of the first Kentucky Convention at Danville, sitting as a delegate from Lincoln County. Squire continued to live at Painted Stone throughout 1785 and part of 1786, but his landowning scheme backfired, and he began to lose thousands of acres through fraudulent land titles. His losses and debts mounted, and he had to sell his Painted Stone property as well as his property in Louisville. Disgusted with land speculation, he left for Richmond, Virginia, where, as a delegate to the State Legislature, he voted and signed Virginia's ratification of the Constitution of the United States.

CHAPTER SIX

HOME AT LAST

In 1787 Squire's land losses mounted, so he decided to get away – far away. With one of his sons, Isaiah, and his cousin, Samuel, he headed south to found a new colony near Vicksburg, Mississippi. Indians broke up the beginnings of the colony, and the trio moved as far south as possible – all the way to New Orleans on the Gulf of Mexico. Squire took up his original trade of gunsmithing and opened a gun shop, which he managed for three years. It was moderately successful, but the Spanish government (Louisiana was not yet part of the United States) closed the shop and confiscated his inventory. Dead-broke and discouraged, Squire headed back to Kentucky.

Daniel, in the meantime, had taken a trip back to their old birthplace in Pennsylvania; now he was heading west again. The brothers, who hadn't seen each other for years, got wind of each others' whereabouts and arranged to meet. How better to spend a reunion then on a hunting trip together through virgin forest? This time, they crossed the Ohio River north of their former stomping ground, into what would eventually become southern Indiana.

The brothers were working their way along Buck Creek hunting game, when, out of the hillside they were climbing, they saw a spring gushing torrents of water. (The flow of water from the spring has been estimated at over a million gallons a day.) Daniel and Squire, always inquisitive

A myriad of columns, pillars, and flowstone formations met the astonished eyes of Squire and Daniel Boone in 1790, when a passageway behind a huge spring they had crawled into opened to reveal a network of passages and chambers adorned with thousands of dazzling formations.

They had explored many caves but had never dreamed of underground splendor such as they now beheld.

by nature, had to investigate the water's source. Behind the rushing water, they discovered a passageway extending back under the hill. They crawled in. Imagine their surprise when, after about three hundred feet, the passage opened, revealing in the flickering light from their torches, one of the most magnificent displays of subterranean splendor ever discovered – tens of thousands of dazzling cave formations highlighted by roaring underground streams and waterfalls.

Of all the caves they had explored, they had never seen anything like this.

Exiting the cave, they continued up the hill. Near its top was another cave opening, but after less than twenty feet, its passageway pinched off. Fortuitously, Squire remembered its exact location, nonetheless. This small cave would one day save his life!

After their hunting-trip reunion the brothers again went their separate ways. Daniel traveled to western Virginia, where he was elected to the State Legislature in Richmond; and Squire went to St. Simons Island in Florida*. Squire was seeking a milder climate for relief from the pain of his old wounds, which bothered him in the winter. In the summer of 1782, he left Florida for Pennsylvania, and he and Jane (their children now grown and gone from home) lived for the next three years near Squire's birthplace.

Never one to stay put in the same place for many years, Squire returned to Shelby County, Kentucky, in 1795, where he lived until 1799. Once again he joined Daniel in another adventure. Daniel yearned for a new frontier – one further west. He decided to try Missouri. Of course Squire was ready to go along. Squire and Daniel settled in Missouri on the Quiver River and began to build a stone house. After two

---

*Although Squire always said the island was in Florida, it is actually north of the present state line in Georgia.

An artist's conception of Squire swinging into the cave on a vine to elude pursuing Indians. The cave kept him hidden, and he considered it "Holy Ground." At his request he was buried in this cave upon his death in 1815. This picture first appeared in the Magazine Section of the Sunday Courier-Journal *newspaper in Louisville, Kentucky on June 5, 1938. It illustrated a story titled, "How Squire Boone's Life Hung On A Stunt With A Grapevine."*

years, two of Squire's sons came on out to visit him and looked over the country, but they didn't like it as well as their home. They persuaded their father, now 57 years of age, to return with them to Kentucky's Shelby County.

Having returned to Kentucky, Squire found that his land holdings had virtually evaporated. Back taxes were due, and unscrupulous land attorneys, labeled "land sharks", had taken title to his properties. On May 18, 1804, Squire was so destitute and ashamed that he said he was "principled against going into the town of Shelbyville upon any business whatsoever." A few days later the proud defender of the wilderness, this noble, unscrupulously honest, Christian pioneer, was thrown into prison in Louisville for non-payment of debts. But he was soon released by friends who came to his rescue and paid off his debts.

Squire was now determined to leave Kentucky forever, and he did! This time he didn't go far. The cave he and Daniel had discovered across the Ohio River still haunted his thoughts. The huge spring pouring out of the hillside could power a gristmill. He decided to check out the valley near the cave again, but as he approached the area, the story of his life reoccurred: he was set upon by a band of hostile Indians. Remembering the exact location of the cave entrance near the top of the hill (one old history book terms it "a lofty peak"), and with the Indians in hot pursuit, he swung on a stout vine into the cave, quickly covered the entrance with branches, and began to pray earnestly that he would not be found. The Indians, evidently unaware of the cave, failed to find him. If they had, Squire would have undoubtedly perished on the spot.

He could hear them trampling about, searching for him, but the branches kept him well hidden. Finally they gave up and left. Squire praised his Creator that his prayers

The opening in the ground to the left of the monument is the mouth of the cave into which Squire Boone swung on a vine to hide from pursuing Indians.

The legend on the front of the monument tells the story of his escape, which happened more than two centuries ago.

were answered, and he ever after considered the small cave to be "Holy Ground." He returned to that cave time and time again to pray, meditate, and carve the cave walls with designs and verses of gratitude.

He knew that this was the place where he wanted to live, and in 1804, he made his final move, uniting his entire family. Squire, Jane, their daughter Sarah, and their sons Jonathan, Moses, Isaiah, and Enoch, all moved to the beautiful valley by the cave, which is now near the town of Corydon — Indiana's first state capital. Here Squire, with his entire family, as well as his cousin Samuel and his family, built a village, where Squire lived out his days. They lived peacefully in Squire Boone Village for the final eleven years of Squire's life. This was the longest time he ever stayed in one place. After a lifetime of moving to a different location every one, two, or three years, Squire had at last found the place where he wanted to spend the rest of his life and put down his roots for good.

These were happy years. Squire and his sons set about building a gristmill. It took them nearly four years to complete it, and in 1809, "Boone's Mill" was ready for customers. Squire and his sons ground not only their own grain, but that of the pioneer settlers throughout the valley.

In 1813, just two years before Squire's death, he and his son, Moses, built the first Baptist Church in the state of Indiana. It was located several miles from the village, and was called "Old Goshen." Although Indians often stared in the windows during services, they never bothered Squire or his congregation. The Old Goshen cemetery, near Laconia, Indiana, is the final resting place for many Boone descendents, but not for Squire.

After the new church was completed, he grew weary. He had developed dropsy, or heart failure. He sensed that

Photograph Courtesy of Frederick P. Griffin

"Old Goshen", the first Baptist church in Indiana, built by Squire Boone and his son Moses, in 1813, just two years before Squire's death.

Interior view of Old Goshen showing the hand-hewn pews. This picture appeared in the Rotogravure section of the Indianapolis Star *newspaper on September 13, 1931.*

Old Goshen monument

(Corydon Democrat *Photo*)

A tribute in granite to Old Goshen Church was erected by Squire's fifth cousin, Ray Boone, after the church was razed in the 1960's. The church has now been rebuilt by the State of Indiana. Many Boone descendents are buried in the graveyard next to the church.

Above: Squire Boone's original mill wheel, which had fallen into disrepair after the mill was closed in the early 1900's.

Left: The restored mill wheel as it appears today, again grinding grain at Boone's Mill in Squire Boone Village near Corydon, Indiana.

his life was ebbing. He began fashioning his own coffin out of native walnut growing near the small cave up the hill. Then, from his deathbed he called his sons to his side.

"Promise me," he pleaded, "that you will bury me in the cave where the Lord spared my life from the Indians." His sons agreed.

On August 15, 1815, Johnathan, Moses, Isaiah, and Enoch Boone fulfilled their father's last request and placed him in the coffin he had prepared, carried it up the hill into the cave, and sealed the entrance with a boulder.

For the next one-and-one-half centuries, Squire Boone slept in the cave where he fervently believed the Lord had spared his life from the Indians.

Over the passage of time the walnut coffin rotted in the damp cave, and Squire Boone's bones rested on the cave floor. Silt from the outside washed into the cave during storms, and buried the bones under several feet of dirt. Persons who visited the cave in later years assumed that the bones had been removed, either by relic hunters or by the family for reburial elsewhere, but such was not the case.

In 1973, the large cave behind the waterfall was opened to the public. New entrances had been blasted into Boone's Mill Cave, which was renamed Squire Boone Caverns. Concrete walkways, handrails, and indirect electric lighting were installed. Tens of thousands of tourists came to visit the cave full of glistening formations, rushing underground streams, and shimmering waterfalls.

The first year the cave was opened, an elderly native of the valley, Elmer Wiseman, dropped by and engaged the tour guides in conversation. He casually mentioned that as a lad in the late 1800's he had visited the burial cave with his

Discovery of Squire Boone's bones

Tour guides Allen (left) and Rick Conway, excavating for wall carvings, were astounded to discover the bones of Squire Boone. Rick holds the upper arm bone which was broken and mended crooked, causing one of Squire's arms to be shorter than the other.

Rick Conway holds the skull of the old pioneer, which he unearthed inside the cave.

father and remembered seeing not only pieces of the coffin, but inscriptions Squire had carved onto the cave walls, where he often went to pray and meditate.

Two of the guides, who were brothers, determined to dig out the cave which was filled with silt and debree, in an effort to locate the carvings. They worked at the task in their off-hours for many months. No wall carvings were ever found, but small pieces of rotted walnut were turned up – then small bones – then larger bones — and then a skull. The guides were astounded.

Anthropologists from the University of Louisville were called to the scene, but could not authenticate the bones. Carbon dating was impossible, they said, because the bones had lain in mud and rainwater for so many years. But an unexpected authority appeared. Dr. Milton May, a retired physician and surgeon, then living in Laconia near Squire's Old Goshen Church, himself a descendent of Squire Boone, asked to examine the bones.

He found the upper bone of the right arm of particular interest. "Whosever arm this was had it broken, and it mended crooked," he explained. "This arm would have been shorter than the left one," he went on. Then he examined the skull and looked for an indentation or hole where a toma-hawk might have penetrated. There it was! A hole in the skull right at the place where the tomahawk had wounded Squire at Fort Harrod. Dr. May, long familiar with the battles and wounds of his ancestor, looked up from the table where he was examining the bones and exclaimed, *"Don't ever let anyone tell you that this is not Squire Boone!"*

Another Squire Boone Caverns tour guide, Frank Stephens, who was a retired finish-carpenter, fashioned a walnut coffin. Dr. May's wife, Margaret, also a descendent of Squire Boone, knitted a shroud and embroidered it with

Squire Boone lies in state in 1974 prior to his reburial. His bones were in a shroud knitted by Margaret May, one of his descendents. A new walnut coffin was fashioned by Squire Boone historian Frank Stephens.

Squire Boone now rests within the cave he and his brother Daniel discovered in 1790. The monument was erected by the Daughters of the American Revolution. Both Squire and Daniel were made Honorary Army Captains in the Revolutionary War by a Special Act of Congress.

74

Squire Boone's name and dates of birth and death. The bones were placed in the shroud, which was placed in the coffin, and the lid was sealed with wax. Four pallbearers carried the coffin deep into Squire Boone Caverns where it would no longer be subjected to rain and silt seeping in.

Squire Boone historian, Ted L. Igleheart of Shelbyville, Kentucky, gave a eulogy. Rev. James Pyles preached a short funeral sermon, closing with a prayer. Squire Boone had again been laid to rest. Visitors to Squire Boone Caverns pause at the grave of the old pioneer to hear the tour guide tell the stories of his incredible adventures.

Squire Boone's
beautifully crafted corner cupboard

Photograph by Mike Tonegawa

Photograph by Mike Tonegawa

Left: A corner cupboard Squire Boone built in 1799. Note the fine detail. Squire was a skilled woodworker, who also built the mantlepieces in Daniel Boone's Missouri home.

Above: Squire carved his name and date on the inside of the lower left door. The corner cupboard is privately owned and was acquired from a descendent of Squire Boone.

CONCLUSION

The noted Squire Boone historian, Dr. Willard Rouse Jillson, eloquently summarized the incredible adventures of this noble frontiersman in an address before the Filson Club of Louisville on March 2, 1942, in which he said the following:

"With his older brother Daniel, Squire Boone was given standing as a Revolutionary soldier-officer by Congress in 1813. This action by the National Assembly speaking for the American people was entirely appropriate, for Squire had valiantly served throughout the Indian wars attending the settlement of Kentucky. During the most trying years of this sanguinary period—1779 to 1784—he built, occupied, and, as the elected Captain of a company of frontier militia, defended one of Kentucky's most important and formidable stockaded outposts—The Painted Stone Fort. His personal record in these desultory but continuous Indian wars, which were, in fact, for many years the American Revolution in the West, is perhaps incomparable in leadership and personal combat.

His career as an Indian fighter began in the fall of 1769 when, without a guide, he brought relief to Daniel in the heart of the Kentucky wilderness after his escape from his first Indian captivity. He fought the Indians in bloody battles on the headwaters of the Clinch River in 1770, in Powell's Valley in 1773, at Twetty's Fort in 1775, at Harrod's Fort in 1777, at Fort Boonesborough in 1778, at the Painted Stone in 1780, 1781 and 1782. He was severely wounded eleven times, the scars and crippling of which he carried throughout the remainder of his life. On several occasions, notably at Fort Boonesborough and Fort Harrod, he fought bloody hand-to-hand encounters with Indians, always besting his crafty and audacious opponents. While others about him in these engagements fell beneath the tomahawk and scalping knife of the savage, his skill and prowess sufficed to meet the rapidly changing exigencies of each sanguinary battle. Frequently shot in the body and limbs by Indian rifleball, he always managed, no matter how hard-pressed or difficult the situation, to escape impending captivity. This perhaps, as much as any other achievement of his career, may be seen as an index to his superior mentality, character, and personal endowments.

In August, 1815, in his 71st year, Squire Boone died, and was buried by his request in a cave in which, legend says, he had once taken refuge to escape the pressing attack of a band of scalp-hunting savages. This cavern may be seen today on an Indiana hillside two to three miles north of Brandenburg, Kentucky. A well authenticated tradition has it that when Squire realized that his end was approaching he gathered his children to him and then gave expression to his interest in the possibility of proving life after death. Indicating his desire to be buried in the natural tomb he had selected, he caused his sons to promise to wait at the mouth of the cavern for several hours after his body had finally been laid there to rest. True to their word his sons after laying all that was mortal of their beloved parent in the cave, waited throughout the night at a camp they made on the slope just beneath the entrance to the rugged tomb, but received no communication from their father's departed spirit.

So passed Captain Squire Boone onto the long out trail of life. Early explorer of the West, Indian fighter, pioneer, preacher, border statesman and leader of important settlements in Kentucky, Missouri and Indiana, though he missed somewhat the popular acclaim accorded to many of his contemporaries, particularly his elder brother Daniel, he was in his own right a brave, resolute and God-fearing man whose special capabilities of mind and body made it possible for him to serve with much distinction in a number of fields which has added much luster to the name of Boone on the beginning pages of the history of the frontier."

Appendix A
Squire Boone's Homes

Chronological Order	Location	When He Lived There	His Age When He Lived There
1	Near Reading, Pennsylvania	1744-1747 1759-1764 1792-1795	Birth to 3 15-20 48-51
2	Near Harrisonburg, Virginia	1747-1749	3-5
3	Yadkin River Valley, North Carolina	1749-1759 1764-1775*	5-15 20-31
4	Fort Boonesborough, Kentucky	1775-1777 1778	31-33 34
5	Fort Harrod, Kentucky	1777 1779 1782-1783	33 35 38-39
6	Painted Stone Station and Shelby County, Kentucky	1780-1781 1784-1786 1790 1795-1799 1801-1804	36-37 40-42 46 51-55 57-60
7	Richmond, Virginia	1782 1786	38 42
8	The Falls of the Ohio, (Louisville) Kentucky	1779-1780	35-36
9	Vicksburg, Mississippi	1787	43
10	New Orleans, Louisiana	1787-1790	43-46
11	St. Simons Island, Florida (Georgia?)	1790	46
12	Quiver River, (Defiance) Missouri	1799-1801	55-60
13	Squire Boone Village (near Corydon, Indiana)	1804-1815	60-70

*During these years, Squire was often gone from home for a year or more at a time on expedition trips, usually with Daniel.

Chart: Andy Markley

Appendix A
Squire Boone's Homes

Present day state boundry lines are shown for reference only.

Squire Boone's forts and homes in central Kentucky and southern Indiana

Map: Andy Markley

Fort Boonesborough–Near Winchester, Kentucky

84

Fort Painted Stone–
Near Shelbyville,
Kentucky

Fort Harrod–
Near Harrodsburg,
Kentucky

Boone's Mill
at Squire Boone Village–
Near Corydon Indiana

APPENDIX B

Memorials Pertaining to Squire Boone
Open to the Public

 Original homestead where Squire Boone was born in 1744—near Reading, Pennsylvania

 Pioneer log cabin where Squire Boone first lived in the Yadkin Valley—near Mocksville, North Carolina

 "Squire Boone Rock" dated 1770—in the Courthouse lobby at Richmond, Kentucky

 Fort Harrod—at Harrodsburg, Kentucky

 Fort Boonesborough—near Lexington and Winchester, Kentucky

 Squire Boone Caverns and Village, where Squire lived from 1804 until his death in 1815. Includes his cave, his mill, his carvings, and his grave. Near Corydon, Indiana and Louisville, Kentucky

 Old Goshen Church—near Laconia, Indiana

Squire Boone's Birthplace

Photograph by Father Ralph W. Beiting

Squire was born in this home in 1744. The original was a two-story log cabin to which a stone section was added. After Squire moved away at age three, the log section was taken down and another stone section added. Administered by the Pennsylvania Historical and Museum Commission.

2 Squire Boone's First Home in the Yadkin Valley

Replica of the Boones' first log cabin in North Carolina's Yadkin Valley. Both Squire and Daniel lived here. Located in Daniel Boone State Park.

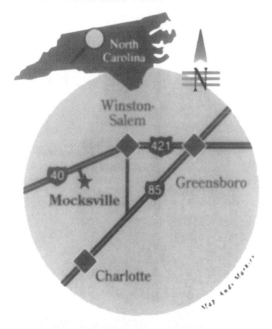

"Squire Boone Rock"

Some historians believe Squire carved this rock as a
signal to his brother Daniel. It is on display in the lobby of
the courthouse at Richmond, Kentucky.

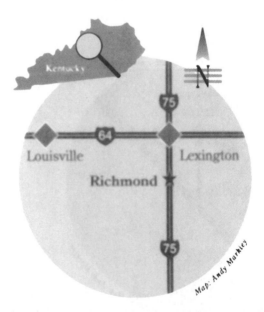

Fort Boonesborough

Fort Boonesborough, a Kentucky State Park, features reconstructed log cabins inside the fort, with many interesting demonstrations of life in the fort in the 1770's. A splendid orientation film is shown.

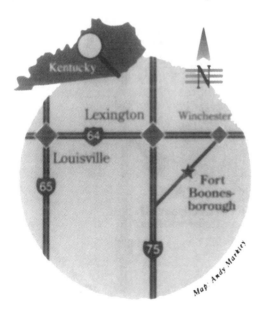

Fort Harrod

Squire Boone and his family lived at Ford Harrod at various times from 1777 through 1783.

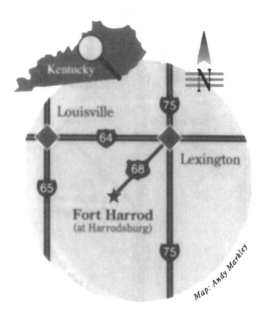

Squire Boone Caverns & Village

Squire Boone lies in state deep within his beloved cave, just as he requested. His gristmill, using the water flowing out of the cave, still grinds grain just as it did nearly two centuries ago when Squire was the miller.

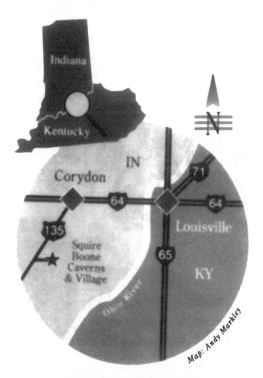

Map: Andy Markley

93

Squire Boone
Village

Near
Corydon, Indiana

1. Cave cabin
2. Manmade cave entrance
3. Natural cave entrance
4. Boone's Mill
6. Village Bakery
7. Soap making
8. Candle making
9. Picnic area
10. Shelter house
13. Boone's Falls
14. Rock and mineral shop
15. Nature trail
17. Traveler's Rest
18. Candy shop
19. Burial cave

Candledipping at Squire
Boone Village

Soapmaking at Squire
Boone Village

Inside view of Squire
Boone's Mill

One of Squire's direct
descendents

APPENDIX B

INDIANAPOLIS, 46204

DEPARTMENT OF NATURAL RESOURCES

JAMES M. RIDENOUR
DIRECTOR

Division of Historic Preservation
and Archaeology
202 North Alabama Street
Indianapolis, Indiana 46204

April 15, 1983

Squire Boone Caverns, Inc.
P.O. Box 411
Corydon, Indiana 47112

Gentlemen:

I am pleased to tell you that the original foundation of the mill, and the
reconstructed mill, located south of Corydon off Highway 135, were listed on
the Indiana State Register of Historic Sites and Structures on December 15,
1982.

The Indiana State Register was authorized by the General Assembly in 1977
(P.L. 163, I.C. 14-3-3-3.3), and is administered by the Indiana Department
of Natural Resources. The State Register is a list of sites, districts,
objects, and buildings, that are significant in the development of Indiana
and local history, architecture, archaeology and culture.

Listing on the State Register provides a measure of protection from State-
funded or assisted construction projects. It places no limitations on what
owners may do with their properties.

If you have any questions concerning the State Register, please contact the
Division of Historic Preservation and Archaeology, 202 North Alabama Street,
Indianapolis, Indiana, 46204.

Sincerely,

Nancy J. Long
Architectural Historian
Division of Historic Preservation
and Archaeology

NJL:jdh

Old Goshen Church

Squire Boone, his son Moses, and other family members built this church—the first Baptist church in Indiana—in 1813, two years before Squire's death. It is located near Laconia, Indiana, several miles from Squire Boone Village.

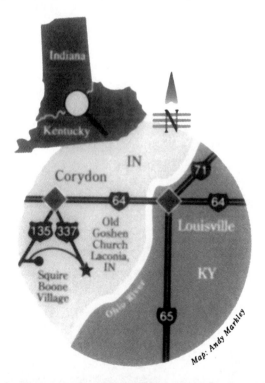

Map: Andy Markley

99

APPENDIX C

AN INTERVIEW WITH 100-YEAR-OLD "UNCLE BOBBY"

One-hundred-year-old "Uncle Bobby" was sitting on the back porch of his home in Corydon, Indiana, when this interview was conducted by a newspaper reporter many years ago. Uncle Bobby was the son of the Negro slave Adam, who was the only survivor of the massacre on October 10, 1773, when Indians captured, tortured, and murdered six young men, one of whom was Daniel Boone's seventeen-year-old son James. Only Adam escaped, and he had often told the story to his son, the subject of this interview.

Uncle Bobby's account of the circumstances leading to Squire Boone's flight to his burial cave to escape Indians differs somewhat from the version generally accepted by most historians. Yet, Uncle Bobby would have had no reason to distort the facts. Perhaps his version is the correct one after all.

"I heard my father tell time and time again about the starting off from Carolina. There were only two Boone families, belonging to Daniel and Squire. A lot of young men went along, and they drew some cattle and horses. In camping out one night some of the cattle strayed away, and seven of the young men, among them my father and Daniel Boone's oldest son, a lad of seventeen, went back a little to look for them. They didn't see no danger because they hadn't seen no Injuns, and pap said they were careless about keeping a

101

watch. All of a sudden a lot of Injuns jumped onto them out of the bushes, and six out of the seven were tomahawked. The Boone's heard the crack of the rifles and came running to help, but it was too late – none escaped but my father.

I could tell you tales about Injuns that would make your hair stand on end in the dark – but I started out to tell you about Squire Boone's last resting place. The Boones and others went down to Blue Licks somewhere roundabout Boonesborough to guard the salt makers. They had been there about a month when the Injuns swarmed out of the bushes and overpowered them with muskits and hatchets. The Boones started to run. Daniel looked back as he heard an Injun yell close behind and seen Squire fall and a big Injun standing over him with a scalping knife in his hand. The news that Squire Boone was killed passed round and most people believed that Squire Boone was killed and scalped by the Injuns. Daniel believed that for months. The Injuns carried him down here (Corydon) and cured his hurts. This was a wild place, full of wild animals and wild men.

The Injuns of the north and the south of the Ohio River were always on scouting expeditions, hunting other Injuns, along with bear, deer, and turkeys, and every trail was a warpath. They had a great respect for Squire. He was a great hunter, and they allowed him to go hunting with them, but they kept a watch on him all the time. For months he lived with them so quiet and contented that the Injuns hoped he would join their tribe. But one day when on a hunt with three Injuns he took a sudden notion to leave them. They called to him, but he ran like a deer – throwed his gun away and ran for dear life.

But they were gaining on him sure and certain. A few hours before in looking for game, in passing along the eastern bluff of Buck Creek, Squire Boone seen a cave-like opening in the rocks almost hidden by bushes. He peered into it and it seemed to be a good hiding place for large game. Now he ran for this cave and reached it when the Injuns weren't a hundred yards behind him. He ran down the steep bluff, tore aside the bushes and entered the cave. He heard the Injuns talking as they passed over his head.

His friends received him as one come from the dead. In telling of his escape, he said that the cave saved his life, and that after his death he wanted to be buried in it.

This Kentucky was a favorite haunt of the Injuns – good rich soil and good water everywhere. Squire Boone observed its good points and thought it a good place for white man, too. So later on he came back, bought a section of government land, built a house and mill out of the limestone with his own hands, and brought his family and spent the rest of his life here. He lived right where pap an I come here to Corydon. It was the capital of Indiana territory, and I seen the legislators at their table in Billy Boone's tavern. He was the oldest son of Squire Boone.*

I come into Indiana Territory when I was eighteen. I've thought many a long hour about the fortunes of the Boones. West and northwest of Laconia there are four small creeks which, after gathering up the surface water for miles, suddenly sink into the ground. This same water goes along under the ground for about two miles and then bursts out of an opening in the limestone bluff of Buck Creek in sufficient quantity to turn an old fashioned overshot wheel and mill. The big cave spring pours a torrent down the hill, falling eighteen feet.

There is Boone's Mill. The stones in it are ornamented with figures and emblems. A trailing vine in full leaf and full

---

*Here Uncle Bobby is in error. Squire never had a son named Billy. This was likely one of Squire's cousins, a son of Samuel Boone.

of fruit was cut into the blocks of stone; and deer, fishes, a cow, a human face and stars, and texts from the Bible. Over a doorway were these words cut into the stone: "The Traveler's Rest, consecrated by Squire Boone, 1809." Over another door is a line from a hymn – "I set 'an sing my soul's salvation, an' bless the God of my creation."

It ain't been such a long time since I was down there. A stone covers the opening in the hillside. We took it off and went down a passage for about seven feet, which led into a room six by eight feet and about five feet high. The coffin had gone to pieces and the bones were exposed. They showed that Squire Boone had been a powerful man, considerable over six feet in height. It seems like something ought to be done to keep people from carrying off the bones, as I heard of a man taking one.

When I think of the dangers, the toil and hardships that the poor man endured alongside his famous brother, as told to me by my father, I think Kentucky owes another duty to the memory of Squire Boone.

BIBLIOGRAPHY

Barnes, Bertha   *Daniel Boone*
        Modern Litho-Print 1971
Beiting, Fr. Ralph W.   *Soldier of the Revolution*
        Modern Litho-Print 1971
Funk, Arville L.   *Squire Boone in Indiana*
        Adams Press 1974 (revised 1978)
Harrod, Rufus C.   *Pioneer Forts and Stations*
        The Shelby News 1967
Hill, George Canning   *Daniel Boone The Pioneer Of
    Kentucky*
        Edward Canning 1859
Hodgkin, Jack K.   *Daniel Boone - The Establishment of
    Fort Boonesborough*
        Kentucky Turf 1974
Igleheart, Ted. L.   *Squire Boone Did Much To Settle
    Kentucky*
        The Shelby News 1967
Jillson, Willard Ruse, Sc.D.   *Squire Boone*
        The Standard Printing Co., Inc. 1942
Lofaro, Michael A.   *The Life and Adventures of Daniel
    Boone*
        The University Press of Kentucky 1978
Moores, Charles   *Old Corydon*
        Indiana Magazine of History March 1917
Ranck, George W.   *Boonesborough*
        John P. Morton & Co. 1901
Robinson, Clifford   *How Squire Boone's Life Hung On
A Stunt With A Grapevine*
        Louisville Courier-Journal Magazine Section
        June 5, 1938
_____ *History of The Falls Cities And Their Counties*
        L.A. Williams & Co. 1882
_____ *Daniel Boone*
        Family Magazine, Cincinnati, Ohio 1836
_____ Various Articles Louisville Courier-Journal
        newspaper
_____ Various Articles Louisville Times newspaper
_____ Various Articles Indianapolis Star newspaper

ACKNOWLEDGEMENTS

The author wishes to thank Frederick P. Griffin, official historian of Harrison County, Indiana, for access to his voluminous files on Squire Boone, which included the Uncle Bobby interview.

The late Frank Stephens of Laconia, Indiana, was an avid Squire Boone historian who traveled thousands of miles in his quest for information and lore pertaining to Squire Boone. Before his death, he spent hours sharing his findings with me. He was a fine man of sterling character.

The late Father Ralph W. Beiting, founder of the interdenominational, non-profit Christian Appalachian Project headquartered in Paintsville, Kentucky, authored a splendid book titled *Soldier of the Revolution — a new view of Daniel Boone*. Father Beiting graciously permitted the use of several excellent photographs from his book for inclusion in this book about Daniel's brother.

Claudia Yundt and her entire staff at Squire Boone Caverns and Village were wonderfully cooperative and even allowed a cavern tour to be interrupted during the photography of the grave inside the cave.

It is my hope that Squire Boone would be pleased with this account of his life. One day, when my days are also ended, I hope to meet him.

W. Fred Conway, Sr.

INDEX

INDEX

INDEX

ABOUT THE AUTHOR

W. Fred Conway, Sr.
December 6, 1929 – September 13, 1999

W. Fred Conway was a southern Indiana industrialist whose hobby was researching and writing history books which shed new light on the subjects. His other titles include *Young Abe Lincoln – His Teenage Years in Indiana*, and *Corydon – The Forgotten Battle of the Civil War*. He also authored books about firefighting lore and early fire engines.

Mr. Conway was a graduate of Duke University with degrees in music and English. During his life, he amassed a collection of antique fire engines and equipment that offers a fascinating visual history of firefighting in the United States. His collection is on display at the Vintage Fire Museum in Jeffersonville, Indiana.

In 1971, Mr. Conway bought the property where Squire Boone Caverns are found. His research led him to discover Squire's love for the caverns and surrounding land where he lived and thrived until his death in 1815. Awed by their beauty and majesty as well as their historical significance, Mr. Conway opened the caverns to the public for all to enjoy.